SHIMMER

ALSO BY MARK IRWIN

POETRY:

A Passion According to Green. New Issues, 2017.

American Urn: New & Selected Poems (1987-2014). Ashland University Poetry Press, 2015.

Large White House Speaking. New Issues, 2013.

Tall If. New Issues, 2008.

Bright Hunger. BOA Edition, 2004.

White City. BOA Editions, 2000.

Quick, Now, Always. BOA Editions, 1996.

Against the Meanwhile (3 Elegies). Wesleyan University Press, 1989.

The Halo of Desire. Baltimore: Galileo Press, 1987.

ESSAYS:

*Monster: Distortion, Abstraction, & Originality
in Contemporary American Poetry*. NY: Peter Lang, 2017.

TRANSLATION:

Zanzibar: Selected Poems & Letters of Arthur Rimbaud (with an afterword by Alain Borer), forthcoming.

Ask the Circle to Forgive You. Selected Poems of Nichita Stănescu (1964-1979). NY: Globe Press, 1983. Translated from the Romanian with Mariana Carpinisan.

Notebook of Shadows. Philippe Denis. NY: Globe Press, 1982.

SHIMMER

mark irwin

2018 PHILIP LEVINE PRIZE FOR POETRY
Selected by C. G. Hanzlicek

Anhinga Press
Tallahassee, Florida 2020

Cover Image: Sarah Charlesworth, Dar Robinson, Toronto, 1980

        black and white mural print; 78 x 42 in. (198.1 x 106.7 cm)

        © The Estate of Sarah Charlesworth. Courtesy Paula Cooper Gallery, New York.

Design, production: Carol Lynne Knight

Type Styles: text set in Adobe Garamond Pro; titles set in Futura Light

Library of Congress Cataloging-in-Publication Data

Shimmer by Mark Irwin — First Edition

ISBN — 978-1-934695-63-0

Library of Congress Control Number — 2019940474

Anhinga Press Inc. is a nonprofit corporation dedicated wholly to the publication and appreciation of fine poetry and other literary genres.

For personal orders, catalogs, and information, write to:

ANHINGA PRESS

P.O. Box 3665 • Tallahassee, Florida 32315

Website: www.anhingapress.org • Email: info@anhingapress.org

Published in the United States by Anhinga Press

Tallahassee, Florida • First Edition, 2020

In memory of Mary Lou Irwin,
August 13, 1928-March 28, 2018

THE PHILIP LEVINE PRIZE FOR POETRY

The annual competition for the Philip Levine Prize for Poetry is sponsored and administered by the M.F.A. Program in Creative Writing at California State University, Fresno.

2018
Mark Irwin
Shimmer
Selected by C. G. Hanzlicek

2017
Tina Mozelle Braziel
Known by Salt
Selected by C. G. Hanzlicek

2016
Rachel Rinehart
The Church in the Plains
Selected by Peter Everwine

2015
Andrea Jurjević
Small Crimes
Selected by C. G. Hanzlicek

2014
Christine Poreba
Rough Knowledge
Selected by Peter Everwine

2013
Chelsea Wagenaar
Mercy Spurs the Bone
Selected by Philip Levine

2012
Barbara Brinson Curiel
Mexican Jenny and Other Poems
Selected by Cornelius Eady

2011
Ariana Nadia Nash
Instructions for Preparing Your Skin
Selected by Denise Duhamel

2010
Lory Bedikian
The Book of Lamenting
Selected by Brian Turner

2009
Sarah Wetzel
Bathsheba Transatlantic
Selected by Garrett Hongo

2008
Shane Seely
The Snowbound House
Selected by Dorianne Laux

2007
Neil Aitken
The Lost Country of Sight
Selected by C.G. Hanzlicek

2006
Lynn Aarti Chandhok
The View from Zero Bridge
Selected by Corrinne Clegg Hales

2005
Roxane Beth Johnson
Jubilee
Selected by Philip Levine

2002
Steven Gehrke
The Pyramids of Malpighi
Selected by Philip Levine

2001
Fleda Brown
Breathing In, Breathing Out
Selected by Philip Levine

CONTENTS

THREE

FOUR

ACKNOWLEDGMENTS

Many thanks to the editors of the following periodicals where these poems first appeared:

32 Poems: "And"

Academy of American Poets Website: "In Autumn"

American Life in Poetry, Ted Kooser, ed. "Open" (reprinted)

American Literary Review: "Paint"

The Believer: "Human Lag"

Blackbird: "Brief Sketch from There to Here," "The Chimpanzee"

Boston Review: "Elegy with Forest & TVs"

Conjunctions: "Horizon Not Much Farther than a Holler," "Memory," "Shimmer," "Progression & Zig Zag," "Landline"

Colorado Review: "Eclipse," "Herald"

Copper Nickel: "Emaciated white horse, still alive, dragged with a winch cable …"

Field: "Dissolving Parable," "Open"

Great River Review: "Like trying to reassemble with twine & glue a bird's nest blown …"

The Hudson Review: "Little Transfiguration Suite"

Manoa: "Dedication," "Electric Psalm"

Massachusetts Review: "Human Pageant"

Moon City Review: "What did you do today? How long will it last? Will you remember?"

New American Writing: "In the Mouth," "Reach"

New England Review: "Here," "What a Great Responsibility"

Plume 5 & 7 Anthologies: "Who" "And Now"

Plume 6 Anthology: "Spare Key"

Plume Online: "You," "Words"

Poetry Northwest: "Dear Red," "How to gather it all up," "Or"

Pratik: "Life is a red car," "Uniform"

The Southern Review: "Toward Where We Are," "Voyage"

The Verses: USA Jubilee Anthology: "Consider the fuel"

Sincere thanks to Charles Hanzlicek for his careful reading of my work, and to Connie Hales at Fresno State University for her coordination of the Philip Levine Prize for Poetry, and also to Jefferson Beavers for the book's promotion.

Thanks also to Lynne Knight and Kristine Snodgrass at Anhinga Press for their wonderful work, long-standing presence and dedication.

Finally, I would like to thank David Keplinger, with whom I have been exchanging criticism for many years, and also thanks to David St. John, and Angie Estes, who read and commented on several individual poems in the manuscript.

Special thanks to Paula Cooper Gallery, New York, for the Sarah Charlesworth permissions.

"Emaciated White Horse, Still Alive…" is for Dexter Booth.

"Eclipse" is for Kelly Kordeleski.

"Uniform" is for David Shields.

SHIMMER

On the surface, this verb means only *to notice,* but it carries overtones of *white, bright, radiance, glitter, shimmer.* Within me there was an outright longing for this radiance which is more than any sort of viewing. I will always long for that kind of seeing, which is in Greek called *leukein.*

— Peter Handke, *Across*

… first memory is of light — the brightness of light — light all around.

— Georgia O'Keefe

I was thinking about the remarks my father had once made concerning the human life span, the time we spend alive, minute to literal minute, birth to death. A period so brief, he said, that we might measure it in seconds.

— Don DeLillo, *Zero K*

ONE

WHAT A GREAT RESPONSIBILITY

What a great responsibility to think of things that no longer exist — the tree house
with ladder struck by lightning.

The skyscraper whose floors and ceilings collapsed as people dined above
while below computer terminals and desks flew out the windows.

What a great responsibility to think of creatures no longer here.
The Tasmanian tiger hunted to extinction, or the golden toad that burrowed
in the high cloud forests of Costa Rica.

What a great responsibility to speak of people no longer here. The humming
of blood, muscle, bone, and skin — of ghost bodies and names
still haunting windows and doors.

What a great responsibility to give human form to words, to place safety cones
around parts of speech, especially nouns and verbs in the past
where work will never cease.

What a great responsibility to know that each "I" on the page leans toward the horizon
while the living lie down with the dead.

What a great responsibility to speak of things and people. This boy pulling
on his father's work-gloves, or that kid in April, dragging an old violin
through loose soil till the pear trees bud and flower in an instant.

IN AUTUMN

When within ourselves we feel the autumn
I become very still, a kind of singing, and try to move
like all things green, in one direction, when within ourselves
the autumn moves, thickening like honey, that light we smear
on faces and hands, then touch the far within one another,
something like autumn, and I think when those who knew
the dead, when they fall asleep, *then what*, then what in autumn
when I always feel I'm writing in red pencil on a piece
of paper growing in thickness the way a pumpkin does,
traveling at fantastic speed toward orange, toward rot, when
in autumn I remember that we are cold-smitten as I continue
smearing red on this precipice, this ledge of paper over
which I lean, trying to touch those I love, their bodies rusting
as I keep writing, sketching their red hands, faces lusting for green.

THRESHOLD

That I searched for some first life, a salamander
shaking off light in the tarn's shallow,
that there are trees growing upside down we can't see,
that there's wind still roving these old photos
while a comet's phosphorescent tail floats beyond
and those vultures continue to poke their heads, gorging on the gorse of a deer.
On TV, the toy jets crash through the city's twin towers but the screams
are real, and from one window a body's free-falling comma,
and I say that between what you see and can't say
lies the animate dark like a field of seeds
sprouting to attention. I'm just trying to breathe,
remembering in Ek' Balam when I held a crowing rooster and touched the sun
just that once with my ears, and this is why
each April, I stand in the barn at mid-morning
and evening, staring at those welts of light through rotten slats,
and that incandescent seam, welling up beneath the door.

SHIMMER

A high-rise lobby mirror is lobbing
suited bodies back and forth while ten thousand
blue screens flicker toward a new ocean
we navigate from land, but to throw a window open
with the entire force of your body's not the same as pushing
a power button on a laptop, or a remote
electronic detonator. Watch this in your room
along with the Ilulissat Glacier melting, the portable
become monstrous illusion. Like the man watching late TV
who shoots his sleeping wife. Just a bad dream,
he tells her, then soothes her back to sleep before
shooting himself. The smoggy stars above
the city's flickering lights — fire thrown down and back — just look
from any jet and marvel at the astral make-up, a grave
of aging, prickling light.

PURPLE

Dying, mother says she dreamed me being born once more
so that "I would know." And I keep thinking about those words,
how she smiled, how happy she was to have this second time,
and how after she died, I dreamt this dream, but in the dream,
I was the infant trying to remember carrying her much later, and she
was the tired woman trying not to forget how old one small body
seemed, and in this dream, my dream summoning hers, we both stood
some place beyond desire, and we spoke to one another
in mewling sounds much older than language, and then we heard
another sound like rain and fire at once, and a light rose from this sound
and I could see there was no left, right, top, nor bottom, and the inner
became outer—the blood-red a cloud-far blue. Everything was so far
it became purple, and this was how she knew that I knew in this purple this very purple.

AND

And I could hear people rushing, but were they arriving or departing?
And the rushing was like the wind off the ocean or mountains, and the wind
was warm or cold, and in one place they were adding rooms
to a house, and in another they were taking them away. How
will they enter now you might ask? And the world became one
without names but memory flowed through it like a river
from which the animals looked up as they were drinking. And people
were cutting one another's hair, and many lay down in the grass growing
higher, and they built huts from it that blew in the wind
along with the one word they spoke — *Yes* — and then all the yesterdays
became now, and there was no early or late, and the only question had something
to do with light, as the grass grew higher, and all the buildings and skyscrapers
turned to rock, and all the rocks to sand while the tiny epic of all
this is being written in red within the four chambers of a sparrow's heart.

WELCOME

This model home where you walk into the living room
with clothes on the floor and people sleeping in one
bedroom. You touch them softly on the shoulder
and they wake, smiling like they've known you all
these years, and then they dress and leave while you
stay and become that couple, and though the staged
photos and imitation fruit are annoying, you become
accustomed to them just as other couples will in
the future, and just as some have in the past, back
to the first settlements in Jamestown, Plymouth,
and Salem. — Someone always arriving to live with
something new, but for right now I would like you
to join us. *Please come in.* No need to knock. Make
yourself at home on the couch. There's a cheese platter
and assorted juices. Can you imagine living here?
Your furniture closing the spaces? Your children
swinging in the back yard? Your grandmother's recipe
for lasagna baking in the oven? Look, the windows
are already starting to fog. Please take this book
and sign your name along with the others.

SPARE KEY

Saw the Chartres cathedral at dawn floating on a memory card where a ghost pigeon skiffed from an alcove.

Saw a hound's teeth snap a marmot in two, the front-end wriggling away from the back.

Saw Jill's belly balloon with twins.
                                    Saw a tumor in Annie's breast.

Tonight, the Milky Way's haze seems frozen along the spine of The Swan's cross — Deneb, Sadr, Albireo — a first language we can't touch.

— Nor in the midst of each body, the sacrum and iliac crest. —Of flesh unfinished.

He kept a spare key from all the apartments and houses where he'd lived — 39 — on a ring hung from the wood stove, their bright tongues clacking in winter.

TOWARD WHERE WE ARE

Now light turns the room a deep orange at dusk and you
think you are floating, but in truth you are falling, and the fall
is so slow, yet precise, like climbing a ladder of straw. Now
leaning forward, you open your hands that keep opening. Is
this what *Yes* feels like? Making a shore where no water was?

MAYBE

Maybe for a moment, maybe an hour, maybe the days? — The costumes we wear. I mean
the costumes of faces cast over

our mouths, their ruined words describing — say — a lemon tree
in sunlight, rain, till the emulsion

dissolves. Maybe you'll remember, maybe over trout
in a restaurant among the tang of forks against

knives, or while staring into the blue stadium of a laptop as the space bar
pushes letters apart and a scar

pulls together skin. — Or maybe while a rooster crows through the roster
of years. Outside, the cars, trucks

and bulldozers churn, turning earth into what is ours. Maybe a factory,
a new club or condo. Or maybe

there's something you prefer to remember, its lozenge over and over.
Or something you avoid like steel wool to the hand, realizing

there are an infinite number of pauses in the word *If*
as a friend is being lowered

into the ground of your heart, soppy with mud
and flowers, while a street vendor

hawks warm pretzels, channeling hunger
into the April air.

THE CHIMPANZEE

from another zoo, just transported, clasps one hand
to the cage, tentatively
looking, blinking at jabs of light through trees, before entering

the diorama with its un-
real grass, each blade like the green seconds

crushed within a day's hour. Now the chimp lies in the shape
of a comma, a pause in a sentence having taken

millions of years to arrive. What

would you do? It stood and looked
at dimensionless walls, a veldt pasteled with trees, then suddenly
stopped, the way

a cliff might, then continued the way a child too eager suddenly arrives
at old age.

TWO PANELS

1.

When I was an egg dividing. When I was a soldier.

When I was far. When I was with family, friends.

When I was in France, North Africa, Italy, Romania.

When I was in church. When I ran too late when _____.

When Mom helped pack insulation into the new walls

of our house. When we danced to "Mack the Knife."

When she went to assisted living and we sat

staring at one another. When she was in a wheelchair.

When I was in a crib. When I was too late or early. *When, when,*

its little breath become wind. When she could no longer speak. When

we passed words on paper, back and forth. When the words meant

nothing. When we passed colors. When red. When blue. When

memory dances till *no* becomes *yes*. When

I sing of you. When green.

2.

When inside the body we saw light, its pink through the color of blood.

When outside we screamed, finding the air toward words.

When we learned to walk, swim, drive, leave, and then sometimes return.

When giving, we learned to make light, and when not, how to lose it.

When we were on our knees waiting for news, or when

— unable to forgive — were given blindfolds.

When one with sky we called to our absent parents,

and when in our age we forgot home, but by trying to remember, little by little,

began to return there, as we first did, and were surprised.

BRIEF SKETCH FROM THERE TO HERE

We've come a long way but our departure's still not
begun. It's as when the first westering explorers thought
they could catch the sun always setting beyond
before someone sketched these cities then began to fill all
the people in. — The wilderness that was and *was* and *was.* What
we once saw, now only pictured. You touch the glassy
paper on the postcard where once there were trees. Its sheen
reminds of a lake's small noise where a hawk's height's
reflected. You touch and touch then realize that you
are aging too, that the field, once so vast, gets smaller
as the players grow, holding onto one another, moving
halfway, then half of that till the last stinging inches, then
the seconds fill us like a lake with rain, and dawn and twilight's
twin dresses, always known, gather to lay us down.

OPEN

When they entered the house, which was a very large house
the way a cloud is large, the pages of their story
seemed like cracks in the earth, a man's shirt, or a woman's
blouse, and the stranger in the house told them to make
themselves at home in the house that was not their house,
and told them to write down the three most important gifts
in each of their lives, and then continued to explain how
there were three doors in the house and at each door they must
forfeit one of these gifts, and how the real story always begins
at the third door, where each of them will pause and begin
to crawl, leaving the field of time, where now you pause,
touching the door of this page, wiping away each word, waiting to enter.

ELECTRIC PSALM

May those deer wandering on the blue screen's green
woods find a stream there. May they remain safe
from whistling bullets till bullets become spent whirring
rounds. May kids from the concrete metropolis find those deer,
their gaze a tissue of fear fetched far from video camera
or computer chip till the laptop becomes sheer altar,
for blessed are those who see among circuitry and glare,
those who can tap a letter's key and know its curved
weight the way deer know the angle of trees and the earth's
curve, yet are fooled by a headlight's glare, or know downwind
an arrow's whoosh, and blessed those whose legs don't buckle,
who run till those woods skirt suburbia's pixeled dusk
toward which they gaze then turn back to a darkness
leaking more, a kind of noise or low flickering your eye
catches on the screen, not the snow falling through red
leaves, snow that builds, joining city to woods, but a restless
drone joining antennae to tree, from which the animals turn
farther, their todays toward tomorrows, unblessed their blessed darkness.

TWO

HUMAN PAGEANT

If I could make language simpler I would.
Language says that each word equals something
else, but that's not true. If I could make
language simpler, I would make an invisible
equals sign that extends through each of us
toward the horizon so that once again our houses
would join the trees. If I could make language
simpler, I would abolish consonants so that we spoke
only in vowels, then we could hoot and scree,
whistle, whinny, and chirp, and I would make C
a vowel because it's a torn O, and I would make
Z a vowel because its sound never ends and races
off the page. If I could make language simpler
I would build a vast plus sign amidst us
all, and people would walk for miles to touch its
tall axis. They would place their hands there and begin
to hum until they could feel the wind of distance, then all
things would be equal and the words no longer sting.

HERE

This world with its dollars and smart phones, this world with its
cumuli and muons. This world

with its coupons and pop-up ads — someone always trying to argue something
like a crow in a lemon tree. In grade school

we used to answer *Here* when roll was called. What it meant then
seems so much less than now, here with Mom

at the nursing home, here with the surgeon cutting the melanoma
from my cheek, here with the homeless vet

and his just-rescued greyhound, the intaglio ribs of both glowing
in sunlight. Here's a burrito,

I say. *Here*, that word like a shiny plough blade pulled by a horse
too far away to see. I remember

water, green and high, and the swarm of bees in an alder's branch I cut, tossed
in the pick-up, then drove

to my hives. Here, I said, their brief diaspora over, the queen far in the brood chamber's
dark. *Here*, I say, six months later

to a neighbor, smearing their honey on bread, and here reader, their muted hum like that river's
through the just-now sense of these words.

SUNLIGHT

through a jar of marmalade, or a drop of water

forming. Marathon runners — bunched — leaving the start, sweat opening

within pores, and the quick jelly of blood

coursing through bodies. A handful of gravel thrown

where a hundred silver minnows scatter. The radiance. — Even the minutes,

hours, days. A human life measured in seconds equal to the years

in a geologic era. I say the words — *bee, piñon, apple, deer, bison* — to keep them

from vanishing. Things we keep — the vase from Truro, a fish fossil from Wyoming, some

feldspar intruded with quartz. Each a nail to fix

the past. — Or the way Joyce's diamond necklace made Joyce's death

different: the tiny shards, each facet shining

from the casket. The darkness comes, the darkness

goes. The pie pans and tie pins, the cuff links

and bandages. To say 7 lakes, 4 spades, 3 gold rings, and a 25th

anniversary. The magnificence and danger of numbers. The codices

in glass cases — or the *Bible, Torah, Koran, Bhagavad Gita.* The way we pick them up,

moving toward a center, but realize that it too has

edges. The cicadas' staccato stanzas braiding

limbs and branches. What string

connects the days? — To love, then lose

that feeling through the years. *Ever* this motion, and then a beast

lumbering through some film we call river — waiting, watching

for our bodies, their red current dissolving into green.

Emaciated white horse, still alive, dragged with a winch cable to be slaughtered ...

You must continue to holler this into the YouTube video. — And what
that one eye flickering still registers from sky
between the barn and your screen. *Stop*, I screamed, the long

parameters of that word. *Stop*, I said, till the horse
becomes a house for us all. We live inside the hide
of that archival tent the wind still bellows

wild. *Abracadabra*, I said, to make the whole thing vanish. Sometimes
you need to forget the words

before you can know the feeling. — To push the shovel's tang
polished from each shove

                                      into blue soil. To bury

the horse in earth while the galloping white space between words never stops.

DOMAIN

The grass-green-light greener after rain, and soaked I'm wearing
my best shirt of minutes, hunger huge in me for what? The deer
in velvet, and the clouds, browed, still sun-jabbed and low, thirsty
for earth. — To read an atlas on a pinhead, or in a skyscraper's
one glared window, a city's history. I dreamed a drone hovering
over a cemetery's mourners, then woke to the more abstract
human, but this green is planning something big, something red
in its biding of gray and blue days. To be alive, to feel
pain — cold on the teeth, a sweat bee's sting, a thorn — or to taste one sweet
segment of an orange's sphere. As if someone might ask, "One day
in the world, what was it like?" To have used all 64 crayons when coloring
your parents' house, pressing extra hard with the white one to capture
those blowing sheets on the line. To find domain in the day's
ephemeral wave. To climb a stair for nothing but to stare,
purposeless as a flashlight at noon, or perhaps to find among stars
the Hyades svelte V mapping Taurus' face, and bright Aldebaran
there like a bumble bee driving into a lily's throat, then fifty
years later to remember this like the sudden glow on a peak just
out of reach and always late in its hurry to be once more.
Once we really moved through a landscape, but now the scenery
unrolls lush colors on a screen. Who cares? We have no
luggage and the tired body's been replaced by a slight ache
in the hand when the keyboard's pushed away, but deep
inside each TV a primal fire is burning, and I can feel it,

walking down the street, looking into each of the picture windows.

I'm entering that one's house now, where the dinner guests are no longer

at their seats but under the dark table, the young and old blowing

out candles, and now we're taking big spoonfuls, handfuls of burnt

sugar and flour, and with eyes closed thrust them into each other's mouth.

LIFE IS A RED CAR,

with the top down, revving along with family and friends —
and then someone says, *Hey, slow down*. — To follow
a thread — even a spider's — dangling anywhere
from air. To map desires to be continued later. To walk half way
out onto a pier, or always leave a glass part full of water. That's a good hedge
until the truth saunters in after hiding for so many
years, and then you realize that the word *yes* is never *was*, but a kind
of continual *is* like bees rumbling noon clover, their scent always
sweetness until something steps outside and glimpses you
from a dream. Upon waking, you see this place
on earth is hollowed out and built of praise. The other day a child
showed her cardboard house to a man who got down
on his hands and knees, turning his head like an animal, and entered
each instancing of that world. Why didn't I tell you
this poem is burning in your stick hands, inside
your stick house where the evening sun coats everything
in orange — so how could you know?

CONSIDER THE FUEL

of Milk, our hands hooking
things while our hearts corral. Consider the strings

of language untying our emotions: Mom
drawered in the earth's toffee-dark while an infant's
rhythmic crying courses through June

green. Urgent its blare, its blossom
raw as that plastic bag's lung

collapsed in the roses I tend
to find their hilarious full-blown mouths
clowning as any politician in noon

light, but the crying won't stop and I follow
its stream through yards, alleys, toward
the drive-up bank where the homeless mother leans

in the building's shade and that child
screams like the sun.

SARAH

My friend Bill, the surgeon, lost his daughter, lost her twice
since he was one of the surgeons that worked on her liver. It's
hard to find a liver. There are waiting lists. They found a liver
but it was late and too big, and Sarah had fallen into a coma.
They trimmed the liver during the long surgery where Bill opened
Sarah precisely with his hands through a long incision. I believe
his hands are still holding his lost daughter's liver just as he
still holds the swing set, still in the backyard, when he
was assembling it. — *Swing set, sunset, swing set*. Bill and I met
through our daughters who used to swing on the swing set together.
Now I hate the word *liver* and its pinkish-brown color. The liver, weighing
about three pounds, is the second heaviest organ next to the skin. Bill is
starting to develop liver spots on his hands. He didn't have these
when we used to swing our daughters on the swing set that wasn't rusty.

MEMORY

The magnesium flare of lightning
freezing the church steeple and town. We run

and run then walk more slowly toward the statue we'll become.

The room's always cold just before dawn when the ghost appears.
His pills are little ladders where he climbed.

— Candles and sparklers on a birthday cake. Laughter. Smell of burnt
sugar and wax. The fabulous

present for each of us: sunlight penetrating wood, or so deep
into sleep's wool it resembles

cloud. Under a microscope one can detect traces of gold
in the blood. — Marveling, to push

being out of forgetfulness. The swooping head of the black swallowtail
resembles its once

caterpillar face, and where grass borders granite, a name
pooling water shines.

LITTLE TRANSFIGURATION SUITE

Out of the pharmacy the man comes clattering
aluminum crutches far in front and to the sides so
as to lift his twisted body
along the sidewalk where a boy running drops
a can of Sprite the man now bends toward and somehow, on one
knee, hands it back as the glass
doors of the bank — crisscrossing light — toss with the shiny can a sudden
glare, in which the man for a split second gets
up, walks away — like you or me — till the clomp-clomping
begins again. Sometimes I want to praise this planet
inch by inch. The perfect blue
knot of the man's tie, the boy's yellow cap and tow-head mop
of hair, a scent of lemon, and the way
for just an instant, our three hands, sticky, touched.

PAINT

He keeps painting the room white and remembers how
they liked looking at one another but said little. — Once
their hands touched in the pie filling, fresh blackberries
mounded in sugar. He can still smell it baking in the oven
as April snow melted. He keeps painting the room white, extra
paint in the corners where the shadows gather, where the dead
sometimes brush, or in the window cornices. He remembers
her hair, black on the pillow. Black there too. The pillow
he still sleeps on. Beauty, what about it? Toward dusk
he's still painting the room, now losing its contour, floating
like an egg. The brush, the breeze, and the gold light hungry
on one wall. He keeps painting its tint away. The truth is
she floated down from a tall building by the sea. The salt urgent
as chlorine in the eyes. The paint thicker, white on the walls,
the paint dripping all over his shoes invisible now as he leaves.

VOYAGE

When we could no longer walk or explore, we decided to wear
the maps and would sit talking, pointing to places, sometimes
touching mountains, canyons, deserts on each other's body
and that was how we fell in love again, sitting next to
each other in the home that was not our home, writing letters
with crooked words, crooked lines we handed back and forth,
the huge hours and spaces between us growing smaller and smaller.

"WHO"

What a strange word like the beginning of a windy
house. Funny how a mouth speaks from where
it eats. — Words, I mean spitting them toward objects starving
to be mentioned, but let's face it, those things could have
been called by other names. Funny too the way words veil
a page and the white you're really sometimes trying to
get to. Lisa called when the black cat Billy was dying,
head up, taking small breaths next to her pillow as she
held him, listening, speaking on the phone, letting me hear
the shallowing as I spoke his name toward still quick
ears. Something opened there between us I can never name.
Something like flame before there were trees, or houses
winked like stars. Sometimes the words are branches, recalling
saplings, then one day you're older and realize that all the doors
are shadows. — That one, that *one* and that *one*. You can
enter and build a new house farther toward the end, where sleep
appears like a victory, then who will be your guest?

What did you do today?
How long will it last?
Will you remember?

Time, trying to name what has no name. Your Mom's
death. Where you were when it happened. You say, Rome,
trying to capture its monuments, Caesars, churches. To say *now*
and know that nothing remains between you and sky. — When
we had new bodies and eager mouths. When you said *cow, truck, horse*
with the entire force of your body, pushing, wrapping names around
things. — The rope of language and all its fraying strings. *Will you
please, will you?* To return to a childhood house no longer *home*
and be haunted by that word. — To forget words when only the body
moans and the town seems all dust under new snow.

THREE

DEAR RED,

as a rose refolding toward evening. Time
like a whistle, or rust gathering on
the body. Time

like taffy, the kids pulling it now
from their mouths, its pink and yellow
strings one may hold decades later as stone.

*   *   *

You won't notice that the house
is a ship, the family album
a raft, and each of the photos

a smaller one built entirely from each
once, its ounces. Once,

to find the beginning there, then to reach down, touch
where the juice was, where milk from the pulp's
now powdered, its tan going

indigo. Dab it on your cheeks, lips.

*   *   *

Was the morning beginning or evening ending? Sometimes waking's
difficult if you're old and dying or if you're young and tired. Spring
makes it easier. The thirty-year re-occurrences of one iris's
blue, bearing varied tints and dizzying scents. — To be all thumbs
like that.

— The less and less possible accumulates in each
of us. I watched the grass, then trees and woods erupt in you.

      *   *   *

And the rivers made of steel at dusk and all the skyscrapers'
windows laying light down upon them, and all the words long ago
we learned to speak in the dark, the way they course
far beyond us like rivers, and all the words
written in books and those flying along the wires
or microwave towers when we push *Send* and they alight
on another screen and we lean forward, trying to learn what we're
trying to say — through the swift verbs and tall nouns
long past — to one another.

      *   *   *

If you listen closely enough each name rings when a person's gone.

Omega, she said to me, that word the helix of all language, a semblance
of truth and vast migrations, something violet and lingering.

      *   *   *

Coming in from the snow, the blood in our bodies becomes swift
again from heat, a prickling in fingers and toes. Something mortal's whispering
this. — A sudden clearing in the west, dusk and the black beads of flies
against the window's glass, their eyes carrying late rooms of light.

*   *   *

Between what I see and what I'm unable to say is what
I want to write, and to write it so you will believe
is what I tried, standing in a small white house next to a dying

man, while kin from five states walked in the front door, then out the back
to say goodbye. His mother last, lay down beside him,
and the two made a sum no one could add.

*   *   *

I like writing your name in gel pen and watching it dry the way a sheet once did
after we'd washed and held it, stretched tight, like a sail in sunlight between our hands
when you were alive, and how after, we lay down on its white, imprinting it slowly
like these words on the page, and then later went back outside
and our skin turned pink from the sun. Remember how green it was in April
before snow began falling through our lives?

*   *   *

She's becoming *No* now, slowly her body, but the mind still hums *Yes*.
She's becoming No — for a long time now — why we hold her.
No words now, what could they say, calving the dark
where she goes now, low under dusk, the grass's
scent still holding light, now the glow.

                  *   *   *

Between the Zoo of living animals and the Zoo of dead ones
you'll find a mirrored alley of human faces screaming prices,
and a boy, listening — walking down the alley between — begins whistling
louder, louder until all we hear is a whistling rising from the screaming
among a new green, hills that lean toward mountains surrounding
a meadow where blowing fur turns to grass, the grass to straw
with which the boy, braying, forever hungry, builds a blowing house.

For Forrest Gander

HORIZON NOT MUCH FARTHER THAN A HOLLER

What remains unclear grows
clearer. That all this
solitude was good for
something like building a pine
from an abandoned
house's shattered boards. Look
how fast it grows in
shadow, how the pieces summon
far away birds
carrying green needles.

ECLIPSE

My sister and I are eating tomato sandwiches, sliced
yellow heirlooms on white bread
with Hellman's mayonnaise at 1:24 pm near
Paducah, Kentucky, when totality hits. — Light
bruising purple till black-out, then Venus glimpsed
along with two minutes of just-thrown stars, and we are bodiless.
I saw my mother, naked once, while walking back into her bathroom
to get my razor — when visiting. — Quick glance at her breasts
and pubic hair, then shame for where I'd been but could never return.
In 2012, *Voyager I* left the solar system's gravitational field,
entering into intergalactic space, that vast field of void between stars.
I like the cartoon where Wile E. Coyote builds a tiger trap to catch Roadrunner,
but when he thinks he has him, and opens the trap, there's a tiger inside. Sometimes it's scary
what a word will summon, its black stripes chasing after a thing.
When the doctor told me what he told me, I wanted to graffiti his white smock
with a Sharpie. Wanted to whisper into his ear a new word, something made
out of *No*, *Please*, and *Yes*. — What I redact from this body of text you will never know.
As the sun waxed full — like twilight backwards — the tomatoes grew
translucent orange and we started eating our sandwiches
again, hungry for what we couldn't say.

REACH

Like snowflakes those
new boulders after
the flood and one

arrowhead we step
into and out of our
bodies touching

door knobs and keys
locking not what
we want but have—I

strike a match that
sounds like your
name *Richard*

who drove an auger
into stone now sun
breaks through a cloud.

HOW TO GATHER IT ALL UP?

And as the flurried sky cleared, the giant snow-capped trees

turned out to be cell-phone towers, and the bird singing what seemed

a spring song reminded that it was late December, and so, disoriented, we

bought a newspaper advertising where for a limited time only you could get

two queen-sized mattresses for the price of one — or perhaps die

for the single price of living, like that bee — just back

in October — slowed by a near-frost and dazed to a half-crawl

within the tall mouth of a day lily where it staggered among spent anthers.

It reminds how first life is not enough, then too much. — Or of where

we cram things now — on a microchip — or scrunched, with bicycles,

desks, and lawn chairs, into a pod packed with other pods in a large

building. — Now some quick-silver sun through clouds. How to gather

it all up? Or where to go when it's gone? There's always the forest

at midnight, where we *would have* in the past. It waits there untended,

all of its urgent trees, and now those tons of snow you've gained or lost

in sleep begin to form a mountain you must climb, one in memory,

and it's the smell of snow melting in sun that keeps you going.

PROGRESSION & ZIGZAG

To build a tower on the causeway, then a bridge to approach it,
and when the population triples, a tunnel beneath the river, and a high speed
rail from the airport where the jets weigh in and out, uploading minutes, hours, emblazing

the nights, debriding them, our sleep with thousand-beacons
                                                    till it's no longer late or early.

If we could only feel the night sooner, then the breathing darkness might seem
possible, and all the *to*'s and *from*'s would seem like swallows' veering paths,

something fast and slow at once as the dusk light pours continually through glass.

UNIFORM

Coming straight down Magnolia Drive the wheelchair with the vet screaming,
"Com'on, *hit* me, God dammit, *hit* me,"

and he hit my stopped Honda, again and again, blood on one chrome
rail of his chair. "Hit me, *please*," he said, "hit me."

* * *

Samuel Johnson said, "A book should either allow us to escape existence
or teach us how to endure it." Some people I think

are books — like the Jordanian pilot Muath al-Kasasbeh who — dressed in an orange gown,
doused with gasoline by ISIS — was placed in a steel cage and burned alive.

Unrestrained, hopping, smacking the flames on his face,
unable to escape or endure, he finally collapses, every orange page of him wanting to rise.

* * *

                                                        Funny how for a child
objects always seem permanent the way, for an adult, people are not.

Tara, putting on her school blouse, says to her toy-green parakeet, "Never disappear."

Jack says to his stuffed tiger, "*Grrrr, Grrrr*," then hides it in the special drawer.

* * *

There was a light rain on Magnolia Drive and the smell of apple blossoms
connected all the living world. The vet had scabs on his hands

and the wheelchair gleamed in sunlight as the scent of blood mixed with pollen.
Spit hung from his chin. He talked about Khe Sanh, just south
of the DMZ, the chopper trying to lift, mortar fire — and then pulled a piece of green

cloth from his pocket, laughed, and called me a crazy mother fucker. A robin
sang as the world stopped. I remember this so well.

WISH

Make a wish, she said, which seemed strange since *she*

was dying, but I didn't want to make the obvious

one, so I made another. You only get

one wish, she said, so you better make it a good one. We were

old lovers, like chocolate melted in sun, and now

we were trying to eat that chocolate. Desire's

a strange thing, she said. Once when I was a girl I wanted a toy pink

horse because everybody else had one, but then later I asked

my mother to dye it blue. To be free —

to be always arriving, she said, and that was

the last I saw of her. Years later, talking

in a bar, a friend told me the story of some men in South America

trapped inside a mine. He'd just split up with his wife.

He told me there were eight men and one mule. All

the men except one were digging furiously with their picks

and shovels, but the one man just kept whispering

to the mule, grooming it

with a curry-comb, both the man and the animal breathing slowly

while gold sparks whirled about them.

What did you wish? my friend asked, but I was

busy brushing the mule,

listening for whatever opening among the small fires.

HOW MAGIC

Standing in front of a door so large it could be a house,

I see above, the glint of windows that appear like falling water,

and because this door seems too tall to open, I try to write on it

but the letters only spread apart like untethered buoys on the ocean,

and now this house becomes a growing building, and within those windows

I catch glimpses — friends and loved ones — rising, and I want to fire

a cartoon rocket to tell them how magic it's all been, even those quiet terrors

revealed as the sun shone, and I can see the rocket climbing, and all the people's arms

pointing at its fiery-phosphor tail that lighting up the dusk says,

this world was built of praise where our bodies spoke, unlike these words

that sometimes cover up the white with a newer, stranger dark.

FOUR

DISSOLVING PARABLE

In the woods they cut each other's hair and let it fall
just like that, just

like the sashaying yellow leaves they finally lay down on, just
a magic blanket

the earth would eat, and once in the new apartment she lay down
on her open

suitcase of clothes and slept till those clothes were warm, just like she
was getting ready

to walk into the woods and become involved in falling snow,
but not the way

soldiers did in the Ardennes, in 1944, throwing red snowballs, just
like that, just to

pass the lousy time, he told her in the dusk as she
dug with her hands through

snow and the earth where pieces of mica and quartz glittered among
dark roots and stones

and she remembered unmaking the bed when he was inside her, just like that, just
as the sky clearing

became diffuse like a face in memory.

HERALD

A laughter that follows you like a fence and makes
a cage in the failing light till a lock clicks and you miss home, its chimney
staining but speaking to clouds. I remember how guilty I felt
putting sunscreen on the day after you died. — Noon's
glare off snow, bright seeds from the Big Bang. I should have
let it burn my face. How odd to speak
of you *now*, a name glittering off the tongue
into air. Better to speak orphaned words
not clothed in a suit of grammar than to keep foraging
for the dead while the memory fades and words
get stranger, like catkins blown gold, their pollen
roving, a way of rowing back
from death, where *Here*'s mass of jumbled places ends. What
I'm trying to say is that sometimes the wooden
door opens to deer, the deer toward woods, and the woods
toward lumber that becomes a house again where you stand, holding
a shirt like a body, trying to wash the bloodstain out, its tiny waves
like lips or distant, sunset-hands.

DEDICATION

To the alphabet texted through ten million iPhones
or shot through names of the living and dead.
To the letter X that lives between numbers.
To "I" that wants to become 1, and to "O" that lusts for the sun.
To the bees and their furious hexagons.
To the cubicles rising in a skyscraper not beyond
voices carrying a threat. To the echo of footsteps in a stadium.
To him to her to them. To all the screams and glass
splintering back toward windows. To those born
crying, awaiting their names. To the hungry,
shaking seconds out like salt. To the animals that are
numbered. To the churches and slaughterhouses
and to the words that multiply. To those
who push *Send*. To all knowledge finally swept
toward information, then satellite
encoded. To *to,* how it keeps
marvelously opening, and to everyone's eyes
in the digital haze.

ELEGY WITH FOREST AND TVs

1.

— And strung around each Lego-metropolis, the contrails of jets gilding the dawn sky.
Looking down, you can hear a silent chord.

2.

Men surrounded by lumber and nails, then suddenly a house with two kids, a dog, swing set
and barbeque, spinning on its street among other homes
on the green grass of this planet.

                                    And now the net of cell phone calls
tossed out, expanding, joining everyone the way falling snow does, footprints
covered by morning.

3.

                        In spring, if you listen closely enough
you can hear teeth of rust scraping along the gutters. And there on TVs
through picture windows, new American cars. And there
on TVs — diamonds, burgers, and American wars
afloat with flags, SUVs, and Humvees aflame.

4.

How many square feet in a disaster? "Time
to Refi," Bob says to Karen, giving her
a high-five.

           "The other day," he says, "a mattress blew off a pick-up, and a woman, sobbing,
got out and lay down on it, saying 'Fuck you' to all
the honking cars." "I love you

Bob," Karen says, as they walk toward the trail. And there in the woods
a bear carrying an entire city on its back — streets and alleys — twisting, shaking, as it slobbers,
bucking off the roofs of buildings where they rise up in the forest again.

IN THE OPEN

There's the place where the sun strikes you and the place where darkness gathers.

There's the letter you answered and the one you didn't, waiting
in a drawer opened every day.

There's the photo of the face that lived on four continents now enclosed by a frame
just shallow enough to hold the water in your hands.

There's the bed where you sleep, grown wide now, and the ocean
where the house sometimes floats.

There are the swimmers you recognize from another life. Their faces are the same
but their bodies have grown thin as they motion you toward the water,

but instead you return to the house and begin writing to one,
each cursive wingful. *Thank you*, you write,
then to each of the others, *Thank you*.

Those words slap like sunlit waves against the dock. Then you think of the face in the photo
again, when she stood in a field of billowing spring wheat, or waved a ski pole
from a valley of snow and your *Hello* echoed round' the mountains,

as now the water in the picture frame turns to ice. *There is* no dock, no house
on the water, but those swimmers continue to move through your sleep

hollowing something out whose dusk is as wide and violet as the fled years are long.

HUMAN LAG

Mother told me I was born in a dark cabin surrounded by pines

so thick that all day it seemed like evening. Mother said that my

bearded father could not speak and that of his face only the eyes,

nose, and mouth were visible among a lingering scent of creek bed

moss. Mother told me that when I cried as an infant she would take me

into the barn where only the lowing of cows and neighing of horses

would quiet me, but once I saw mother axe off a chicken's head

on a stump, and that chicken pulled a red string twice around that cabin's grass,

a string I knew led into our own bodies, a string I would later

use to pull Mom & Dad around in old age, their human lag.

LANDLINE

Please, I wanted you to hear me. Please, the character
of each word like touching the chains of a swing after
a son has gone. Please, sit down. It's about someone
close to you, the river's engravure, the dug-in trees. Please, are
you sitting down? The gravitas of houses at dusk, or imagine
a panther asleep. You sound so close. Yes, I'm sorry. They
found him in his apartment. No, there's no static now. We once made
a fence of sticks and I remember mooring the boat, tying
a wet shoe, and yes, his horse hitched, that skittish mare. Funny how
as you get older there's less to hold onto. Did you know
there's a seed vault tunneled in a mountain on the Svalbard archipelago? — No
microwave frequency interference. The seeds are sealed in special four-ply
heat-sealed plastic, and the entrance is lit up with highly reflective
stainless steel art so we can find it. Yes, finally each is left
with his or her own energy. I've been reading about orphaned
stars, which makes me still thankful for the grid of utility
lines. *Yes,* face down in the tub. Today, I almost wept for the minutes
to pass. Birds darken the wires during these times when the trees are less.

OR

the quiet and terrifying parentheses of our lives.
I mean deep into the novel, or between
acts of a play. I mean the space around the red
uvula when the scream ends. I mean the packed
auditorium — and the one who threw candy before
another sprayed bullets. Yes, between the two.
Or later, what the pink borders of the dissolving
wound say. And yes, at the nursing home, talking
to your grandmother and then 40 years later to your
mother. Why you were always trying to make
the least sound, as when tending that fire on
the mountain. How the flames and clouds listened
while the huge in-between kept inching beyond.

ROUND

The April wind's pushing clouds to find sun again.
Inside, a dozen clocks are ticking in different rooms.
Some pink shoes, tied by a string, hang from the wall.

The April wind's pushing clouds to find sun again.
Some pink shoes, tied by a string, hang from the wall.
In the backyard, bees swirl up from white hives.

On the dining table an address book lies open.
Many names are crossed out; a few are circled.
In the backyard bees swirl up from white hives.

The bees circle and buzz while the clocks keep ticking.
Many names are crossed out and some are circled
the way bees are with gold and the clocks with ticking.

In the back yard, a white-suited bee keeper bends. Time
makes a canyon from clouds. Sometimes you walk in.

IN THE MOUTH

of mother's death already another mouth's
opening onto a mountain, below which jonquils
yawn in the sun-struck snow
as the hours, seasons
move where a brute bee roves a thistle's
purple castle, dragging pollen doubloons
across the spiked corset's
plume then rests on the bract's
green prong. Mother liked to bake
cakes and hold her breath
under water, to steam windows up
with chicken stock soups.
Mother liked to ask, *How*
will you get on
without me? as she opened her mouth
till the snow
would start falling, *snow,*
snow, the word she would pronounce
so slowly we would fall asleep
in the tall house as she read that story.

WORDS

A dying man whispered in my ear, "You go
now," and I did. — All *here* dissolving into *there*. Now,
years later, I'm taking the black paper off the back
of the photo, the frame, that space where shadow
falls, the invisible woods where I repeat words, climb trees —
space where I tack a piece of foil to transmit still faint
sounds, or mirror blood from a white table cloth, its
small time. — People rushing in and out of doors, rust
collecting from the chain that moved a wheel. June freckles
then sun spots on his skin. — A basal cell, the colossal
hours. Now pushing the picture's edges back down is like leaving
a room, or climbing a mountain. Look, there's snow
creeping down from the glacier and we're blinking against
the bright light, opening door after door with a red knife.

AND NOW

That all these years, traveling toward the page, I was learning
how to make light, to make things visible — hair bound by a tortoise shell clip,
a wedding band whose thousand scratches each comprise a lost orbit,
a fascicle of red leaves, still sun-struck, talking of the charcoal trees, light
leaping from a trout's side, the luck of it, as if there I could find
the spangled surface of eternity. I want the word that's drawn like a thorn
from my finger. No, I want the word *thorn* just as its barb's pulled out,
leaving a prick of blood as I write that word. I want one soap bubble back
from your last bath, and then to stare into its eye, wide-open and astonished
as that of a fish. And now, *once* seems like a long time as I think
how everything's made of atoms, the atom primarily of empty space
where electrons whirl at great speed, even in my hand as I write this, watching
dusk fill the body of a shiny spoon I put into my mouth till I can taste
the whirling of all things visible moving toward what I can't see.

ABOUT THE AUTHOR

Mark Irwin is the author of nine collections of poetry, which include *A Passion According to Green* (2017), *American Urn: Selected Poems* (1987-2014), *Large White House Speaking* (2013), *Tall If* (2008), *Bright Hunger* (2004), *White City* (2000), *Quick, Now, Always* (1996), and *Against the Meanwhile: Three Elegies* (1988). He also has translated Philippe Denis' *Notebook of Shadows* and Nichita Stănescu's *Ask the Circle to Forgive You: Selected Poems*. His collection of essays, *Monster: Distortion, Abstraction, and Originality in Contemporary American Poetry*, was published in 2017. His poetry and essays have appeared in many literary magazines including *The American Poetry Review, Agni Review, The Atlantic Monthly, Georgia Review, Harper's, The Kenyon Review, Paris Review, Pleiades, Poetry, The Nation, New England Review, New American Writing, The New Republic, The New York Times*, and *The Southern Review*.

Recognition for his work includes The Nation/Discovery Award, four Pushcart Prizes, two Colorado Book Awards, the James Wright Poetry Award, and fellowships from the National Endowment for the Arts, and the Fulbright, Lilly, and Wurlitzer Foundations. He is a professor in the PhD in Creative Writing & Literature Program at the University of Southern California and lives in Los Angeles and Colorado. His poetry has been translated into several languages.